GW00647432

AWAKEN TO LEADERSHIP

AWAKEN TO LEADERSHIP

A COMPILATION OF FIVE ESSAYS ON LEADERSHIP FROM A
BIBLICAL PERSPECTIVE

DELORIS S. THOMAS

AWAKEN TO LEADERSHIP

Published by

Word of Life Church International, Incorporated

Suite 1-473

93 Old York Road

Jenkintown, PA 19046

© 2018 by Deloris S. Thomas

ISBN: 978-0-9839527-2-5 (Paperback)

Cover design by: Jerrold Daniels

CONTACT

For more information:

WORD OF LIFE INTERNATIONAL, INCORPORATED

info@wordoflifeny.org

TABLE OF CONTENTS

ACKNOWLEDGMENTS

Thank you to my heavenly Father and the Holy Spirit for the guidance and wisdom given to me to complete this book. Special thanks to my beloved husband, friend, confidant, and editor, Ray for his support and encouragement to fulfill the will of God for my life. I am so thankful to my mother, Judith and my brother, Leonard for their unwavering support and confidence in me. Most of all, thank you to my daughter, Danielle who reminds me that with God all things are possible. My sincerest gratitude to Djuana Daniel, Jerrold Daniels, Teresa Barnes, Clinton Palframan, Ndumi Medupe, my co-workers, friends, family, and Pastor for lifting me up in prayer and encouraging me to keep living by faith.

INTRODUCTION

This book represents an act of obedience to God to write and publish a book on leadership. After months and years of delay and disobedience to the voice of the Lord, I consulted with the Holy Spirit to explain the reasons for the delay. I presented facts about my busy work schedule and life in general. I explained that since God directed me to pursue a Ph.D., he must understand the limited time to commit to writing a book while maintaining a full-time work and school schedule. I clearly heard God's voice commanding me to compile the research articles I prepared for school and publish the book NOW! Essentially, any more excuses meant blatant disobedience to God.

I continued to delay until I received an email from South Africa informing me that on my upcoming trip for work, I am scheduled to speak, and I must provide products for sale. Teresa Barnes encouraged me to complete the book. I knew Teresa heard God and served as an instrument of God to encourage me to do the will of God. The chapters you will read are excerpts from various research papers submitted for assignments for my Ph.D. studies. I edited the essays to present the content in a less scholarly manner but retained some technical jargon in an effort to elucidate leadership theories from a biblical perspective.

In this initial edition of the book, I write about the leadership crisis plaguing our economic, political, and religious institutions. Chapter two outlines the differences between a righteous and unrighteous leader as well as our responsibility to select godly leadership in every sphere of influence. Chapter three highlights the courageous role of a token leader by examining the story of Esther. Chapter four explores the story of Daniel and how jealous and malevolent leaders in organizations seek to harm others by manipulating the decision maker. Lastly, chapter five covers the importance of leaders exhibiting Christ-like virtues such as compassion, forgiveness, humility, and meekness to lead effectively.

To synthesize the information, I conclude each chapter with summary points and exercises to apply lessons learned. The exercises will challenge you to examine your leadership style as well as other leaders and highlight areas needing alignment to the biblical model of leadership. The compilation of the essays challenges readers to become more alert, accountable, and discerning in selecting and functioning as godly leaders. I pray this book serves as a blessing to you and to those you lead.

CHAPTER ONE

LEADERSHIP CRISIS

The people of the land have used oppression, and exercised robbery, and have vexed the poor and needy: yea, they have oppressed the stranger wrongfully. And I sought for a man among them that should make up the hedge, and stand in the gap before me for the land, that I should not destroy it: but I found none.

Ezekiel 22:29–30

Wake up! We are in a leadership crisis. Corporate scandals and malfeasance resulting in the 2008 financial crisis and massive layoffs serve only as a precursor to accusations of sexual misconduct by famed leaders. Researchers believed the economic calamity reflected the lack of values and ethics that led to the inability of the leader to discriminate between good and bad decisions.[1] A leader's decision about what is right or wrong depends on their level of moral development and moral identity. In times past, followers demanded that leaders exhibit character full of integrity, trustworthiness, and decency. The qualifications to earn the title of leader meant surviving the passage of rigorous public scrutiny and verifiable evidence of substantive accomplishments in improving the quality of life for humankind. Consequently, cynicism gives way to a new trend whereby people look for leaders based on the size of social media following, the level of accumulated wealth, tribal ideological affiliations, or simply a person's art of persuasion. Sadly, we must now scour our communities, churches, and workplaces to find at least one adult-in-the-room. The adult-in-the-room refers to the person or movement that decides to take courage and speak up for moral, social, and economic justice worthy of becoming deputized as a leader.

> WE MUST EXAMINE THE SCRIPTURES TO LEARN GOD'S PLAN FOR LEADERSHIP.

Gary Yukl, a noted leadership scholar, explains that "unethical, abusive leadership is more likely for a person who has low conscientiousness, high neuroticism, high narcissism, and a personalized power orientation."[2] The unethical and deplorable behavior of our religious, corporate, and political leaders challenges the confidence, trust, and esteem once bestowed upon our leaders. The Bible outlines leadership attributes and the national consequence of good and bad leaders. From the beginning, the first three chapters in the Book of Genesis depicted Adam as a man who failed to lead. Adam's inclination to succumb to his self-interest led him to abdicate his responsibilities of leadership and obedience to God. He failed to discern and fully comprehend the consequences of his actions for himself and all of humanity.

We must examine the scriptures to learn God's plan for leadership. The Bible outlines the qualifications and the framework for selecting leaders in scriptures such as:

Deuteronomy 17:14–20 New American Standard Bible (NASB)

When you enter the land which the LORD your God gives you, and you possess it and live in it, and you say, 'I will set a king over me like all the nations who are around me, you shall surely set a king over you whom the LORD your God chooses, one from among your countrymen you shall set as king over yourselves; you may not put a foreigner over yourselves who is not your countryman. "Moreover, he shall not multiply horses for himself, nor shall he cause the people to return to Egypt to multiply horses, since the LORD has said to you, 'You shall never again return that way.' "He shall not multiply wives for himself, or else his heart will turn away; nor shall he greatly increase silver and gold for himself. "Now it shall come about when he sits on the throne of his kingdom, he shall write for himself a copy of this law on a scroll in the presence of the Levitical priests. "It shall be with him and he shall read it all the days of his life, that he may learn to fear the LORD his God, by carefully observing all the words of this law and these statutes, that his heart may not be lifted up above his countrymen and that he may not turn aside from the commandment, to the right or the left, so that he and his sons may continue long in his kingdom in the midst of Israel.

Exodus 18:21 Amplified Bible (AMP)

Furthermore, you shall select from all the people competent men who [reverently] fear God, men of truth, those who hate dishonest gain; you shall place these over the people as leaders of thousands, of hundreds, of fifties and of tens.

1 Timothy 3:2–4 Amplified Bible (AMP)

Now an overseer must be blameless and beyond reproach, the husband of one wife, self-controlled, sensible, respectable, hospitable, able to teach, not addicted to wine, not a bully nor quick-tempered and hot-headed, but gentle and considerate, free from the love of money [not greedy for wealth and its inherent power—financially ethical]. He must manage his own household well, keeping his children under control with all dignity [keeping them respectful and well-behaved].

The Sacred scriptures emphasize the importance of selecting a leader with high levels of moral development. Kohlberg outlined six stages of moral development with the lowest level representing a leader's self-interest and at the highest level the pursuit of ethical and moral decisions.[3] Leaders must possess qualities including competence, reverence of God, honesty, the pursuit of justice, and ethical management of resources. Poor leaders fail to attain high levels of moral development and tend to put followers at risk. Isaiah 9:16 noted, *"For the leaders of this people cause them to err; and they that are led of them are destroyed."* Likewise, Matthew 15:14 warns, *"Let them alone: they be blind leaders of the blind. And if the blind lead the blind, both shall fall into the ditch."* Followers put themselves at great risk when selecting a leader and must, therefore, take equal ownership of the current leadership crisis. We must wake up and become vigilant in praying for God's wisdom in vetting and selecting our leaders.

> POOR LEADERS FAIL TO ATTAIN HIGH LEVELS OF MORAL DEVELOPMENT AND TEND TO PUT FOLLOWERS AT RISK.

Jesus represents an exemplary leader, who forsook self-interest and made decisions based on high moral standards. The pericope found in Luke 22:39–46 NASB depicts the narrative about the Passion, an intimate yet intense episode in Jesus' life as a leader.

And He came out and proceeded as was His custom to the Mount of Olives: and the disciples also followed Him. When He arrived at the place, He said to them, "Pray that you may not enter into temptation." And He withdrew

15

from them about a stone's throw, and He knelt down and began to pray, saying, "Father, if You are willing, remove this cup from Me; yet not My will, but Yours be done. Now an angel from heaven appeared to Him, strengthening Him. And being in agony He was praying very fervently; and His sweat became like drops of blood, falling down upon the ground. When He rose from prayer, He came to the disciples and found them sleeping from sorrow, and said to them, "Why are you sleeping? Get up and pray that you may not enter into temptation."

Jesus faced a conundrum and sought direction from God. Jesus knew of His impending arrest and death by way of crucifixion as part of His mission as a leader. He finished the Passover Seder, the Last Supper, and traveled to Mount Olive to pray with His disciples. He instructed the disciples to pray so they may not fall into temptation while he withdrew to engage in an intense dialogue with God. Jesus appealed to God saying, *"Father, if You are willing, remove this cup from me; yet not My will but Yours be done."* Jesus wrestled with the decision to face death in exchange for delivering humanity from destruction.

For context, in Jesus' era, His fame exceeded the popularity of our contemporary leaders such as the Pope, Billy Graham, T.D. Jakes, or Joel Osteen. Jesus' fame threatened the viability of some of the most powerful religious leaders at that time. Jesus performed miracles of healing, manifested supernatural provision, and achieved tremendous victories. Matthew 12:13–15 reads:

> Then saith He to the man, Stretch forth thine hand. And he stretched it forth; and it was restored whole, like as the other. Then the Pharisees went out, and held a council against him, how they might destroy him. But when Jesus knew it, he withdrew himself from thence: and great multitudes followed him, and he healed them all.

Despite Jesus' fame, he resisted the temptation and the lust of His ambition and decided to become a martyr to redeem humankind from sin. Jesus depended upon God and submitted to God's will for His life. Jesus exercised inner strength and courage to acknowledge, trust, and obey God's plan. Also, Jesus held His disciples accountable to also submit to God's plan by directing them to pray. The Bible states that after Jesus finished praying, He asked the disciples, why they fell asleep and instructed them to "Get up and pray that they may not enter into temptation." Jesus functioned as a man as he agonized and prayed continuously about the difficult decision to face His death to save humanity. Philippians 2:7–8 explained, *"But [Jesus] made himself of no reputation, and took upon him the form of a servant, and was made in the likeness of men: And being found in fashion as a man, he humbled himself, and became obedient unto death, even the death of the cross."* Jesus knew that His crucifixion meant possible humiliation, the appearance of weakness as He sets aside His divinity, discouragement to His followers, and a deep feeling of shame. Jesus ignored His stature as He knew that to succumb to the pressure of public perception meant a possible derailment of His destiny and the eternal damnation of humanity. Think about how often we abort our destiny to avoid shame. I recall early in my career; I felt ashamed at the pace of my promotion as I noticed that many coworkers in my cohort received their promotion before me. In fact, I became overwhelmed by the shame and eventually resigned my position and left the firm for a position at another company. Later, I found out that the senior leadership team delayed my promotion because they sought a more prized position for me than opportunities they availed for my peers. The Bible warns us in Second Corinthians 10:12, *"For we dare not make ourselves of the number, or compare ourselves with some that commend themselves: but they measuring themselves by themselves, and comparing themselves among themselves, are not wise."* In retrospect, I realize the lack of wisdom in buckling to the peer pressure, public perception, and shame that led to poor decision-making.

> THINK ABOUT HOW OFTEN WE ABORT OUR DESTINY TO AVOID SHAME.

Leaders must exhibit the emotional stability to make quality decisions. Sadly, a leaders' ambition to climb the corporate ladder and pursue a life of luxury leads to decisions that lay off workers and defraud customers in exchange for large bonus checks and shareholder rewards. Researchers recorded a precipitous climb of executive compensation at over 400 times more than the average worker.[4] Slatter writes that "No amount of moral reprimand or legal barrier is able to extinguish this kind of brash, deep, insatiable, and ultimately mysterious desire for money and possessions, along with the allied aphrodisiac of power."[5] The Bible encourages us in First Corinthians 10:13 that, *"No temptation has overtaken you but such as is common to man; and God is faithful, who will not allow you to be tempted beyond what you are able, but with the temptation will provide the way of escape also, so that you will be able to endure it."* We must follow Jesus and use the transformative power of prayer to face challenges and discern the right solution in difficult situations. Hebrews 12:2 tells us, *"Looking unto Jesus the author and finisher of our faith; who for the joy that was set before him endured the cross, despising the shame, and is set down at the right hand of the throne of God."* Jesus' emotional stability gave him the insight to see the end from the beginning and the courage to withstand the pressure. Begin today by ignoring the shame by developing the emotional fortitude to make quality decisions. In Joshua 1:7 God instructs Joshua saying *"Only be strong and very courageous; be careful to do according to all the law which Moses My servant commanded you; do not turn from it to the right or to the left, so that you may have success wherever you go."* Leadership requires hard work and the courage to make the right choice when faced with a difficult decision.

> LEADERSHIP REQUIRES HARD WORK AND COURAGE.

The unscrupulous leaders of Enron, Arthur Andersen, and WorldCom failed due to the leaders' egos driven to gain notoriety as the largest, fastest-growing, and most profitable business in their industry coupled with complicit lackadaisical employees. The leaders yielded to temptation, and the followers and suppliers fell asleep. A researcher reported that,

> On December 31, 2000, Enron's market value was $75.2 billion, while its book value (balance sheet equity) was $11.5 billion. Arthur Andersen, the auditor of Enron, was the fifth largest auditing firm in the world, employing 85,000 people in 84 countries. On January 10, 2002, they [Arthur Andersen] admitted that they disposed of documents and engaged in the Enron coverup. Worldcom went from being one of the biggest stock market stars of the 1990s to be the largest corporate accounting scandal in the U.S (estimated at $11 billion as of March 2004). Worldcom improperly booked $3.8 billion as capital expenditure, boosting cash flow and profit.[6]

> LEADERS MUST RESIST TEMPTATION BY FOCUSING LESS ON THEIR SELF-INTEREST.

Many of the "Enron employees were subjugated to an environment of fear in the midst of unethical decisions made by key leaders of the organization."[7] Leadership scholars theorize the group behavior of the Enron employees as *Groupthink* and the *Abilene Paradox*, meaning an abandonment of group dissonance. Irving Janis defines groupthink as the "deterioration of mental efficiency, reality testing, and moral judgment" to maintain group cohesion. The Abilene Paradox refers to how a group comes together and decides on a direction contrary to the group's preferred course of action. Essentially, the mounting pressure to not rock-the-boat or to remain numb to reckless leadership becomes a corporate norm. Numbers 13:30–33 King James Version (KJV), describes how failed leadership and groupthink caused fear that resulted in death and the aborted destiny of an entire generation.

And Caleb stilled the people before Moses, and said, Let us go up at once, and possess it; for we are well able to overcome it. But the men that went up with him said, We be not able to go up against the people; for they are stronger than we. And they brought up an evil report of the land which they had searched unto the children of Israel, saying, The land, through which we have gone to search it, is a land that eateth up the inhabitants thereof; and all the people that we saw in it are men of a great stature. And there we saw the giants, the sons of Anak, which come of the giants: and we were in our own sight as grasshoppers, and so we were in their sight. I the LORD have said, I will surely do it unto all this evil congregation, that are gathered together against me: in this wilderness they shall be consumed, and there they shall die.

> FOLLOWERS MUST BECOME LESS COMPLICIT AND BREAKAWAY FROM GROUPTHINK.

The Bible warns of the ill fate of a nation with blind leadership and blind followers. Failure to respond to the unethical behavior and reckless leadership resulted in a global financial crisis, massive layoffs, aborted destinies, and in some cases death. Leaders must resist temptation by focusing less on their self-interest and begin to serve others as a means to protect themselves from their demise. Often leaders face decisions with trade-offs that fall between ambiguous right and wrong choices. A leader's decision to preserve employment for others and forego a bonus differs but resembles the dilemma Jesus faced in giving up His life to save humanity. Jesus endured the cross despite the shame and ultimately received the prized promotion to sit at the right hand of the throne of God. Likewise, followers must become less complicit and breakaway from groupthink and hold leaders accountable for unethical and reckless leadership to mitigate a leadership crisis. Leaders and followers must emulate Jesus and continuously pray to avoid falling into temptation. Wake Up and Pray!

[1]Kooskora, M. "The role of the right values in an economic crisis." *Journal of Management & Change*, 2013: 49-65.

[2]Yukl, Gary. *Leadership in Organizations*. Upper Saddle River, NJ: Pearson Education Inc., 2013.

[3]Ibid.

[4]Evans, J. D., & Hefner, F. "Business ethics and the decision to adopt golden parachute contracts: Empirical evidence of concern for all stakeholders." *Journal of Business Ethics*, 2009: 65-79.

[5]Slatter, M. (2014). The secret life of greed. *Anglican Theological Review*, 96(3), 481-503.

[6]Soltani, Bahram. "The Anatomy of Corporate Fraud: A Comparative Analysis of High Profile American and European Corporate Scandals." *Journal of Business Ethics*, 2014: 251-274.

[7]Turnage, A. "Technological Resistance: A Metaphor Analysis of Enron E-Mail Messages." *Communication Quarterly*, 2013: 519-538.

CHAPTER ONE KEY POINTS

- Everyone must take responsibility for selecting godly leadership.

- The Bible outlines key scriptures as a guide for selecting godly leaders.

- Leaders must exhibit strong moral development to make good decisions in difficult situations.

- Prayer serves as an essential tool to advert temptation.

- Leaders must possess the emotional stability to withstand pressure and ignore possible shame to make quality decisions.

- Godly leaders tend to make good decisions based on the motivation to serve the interest of others over their self-interests.

LIFE APPLICATION EXERCISES

List at least one important or major decision you need to make.

_____

_____

Identify at least one scripture to meditate as you contemplate the decision.

_____

_____

List at least three issues that concern you about the situation?

_____

_____

What personal benefit or risk will result from your decision?

_____

_____

How will others benefit or get hurt from your decision?

_____

_____

THE RIGHTEOUS LEADER

For the Lord knoweth the way of the righteous; but the way of the ungodly shall perish.

Psalm 1:6

The prophet Isaiah highlights the stark contrast between the plight of people governed by an unrighteous ruler and the blessings of a righteous ruler. His prophecies deal with the deliverance of the Jews from their oppressors, the Syrians and the Assyrians, during the reign of King Ahaz. Ahaz functioned as an unrighteous ruler and lacked reverence for God, offered his son as a burnt offering to idols, oppressed Judah, and formed alliances with enemy forces. He turned away from God and imitated the ways of the traditions of the Canaanites. Despite many defeats, Ahaz never turned to God and continued to function as an unrighteous leader. Typically, unrighteous secular and political leaders develop policies that cater to the rich and powerful in society. However, a righteous ruler executes just laws and represents everyone fairly even those with no political or economic clout. A righteous leader operates in integrity and cares for those without the capacity to reciprocate. Across the globe we observe corrupt and unrighteous leaders authoring and endorsing policies resulting in the suffering of many people. Proverbs 29:2 AMPC explains that *"When the [uncompromisingly] righteous are in authority, the people rejoice; but when the wicked man rules, the people groan and sigh."* People and nations prosper and live in safety when the righteous rule.

> PEOPLE AND NATIONS PROSPER AND LIVE IN SAFETY WHEN THE RIGHTEOUS RULE.

Oswalt defines the righteous leader as possessing characteristics of uprightness and faithfulness.

> *Righteousness* is the capacity for doing the right thing in all circumstances and frequently involves keeping one's promises, so that there are times when it may be translated by "deliverance" [as found in Isaiah 51:8] or "vindication" [as in Isaiah 54:17]. *Faithfulness* comes from the root which means to be dependable or true. So, fundamental to both words is the idea of integrity or consistency which results in complete dependability.[1]

The pericope found in Isaiah 11:1–10 ESV prophesied of a new ruler after the miraculous defeat of the Assyrian army. Isaiah declared the reign of a new King, a righteous ruler exercising justice for the vulnerable in society.

There shall come forth a shoot from the stump of Jesse, and a branch from his roots shall bear fruit. And the Spirit of the Lord shall rest upon him, the Spirit of Wisdom and understanding, the Spirit of counsel and might, the Spirit of knowledge and the fear of the Lord. And his delight shall be in the fear of the Lord. He shall not judge by what his eyes see, or decide disputes by what his ears hear, but with righteousness he shall judge the poor, and decide with equity for the meek of the earth; and he shall strike the earth with the rod of his mouth, and with the breath of his lips he shall kill the wicked. Righteousness shall be the belt of his waist, and faithfulness the belt of his loins. The wolf shall dwell with the lamb, and the leopard shall lie down with the young goat, and the calf and the lion and the fattened calf together; and a little child shall lead them. The cow and the bear shall graze; their young shall lie down together; and the lion shall eat straw like the ox. The nursing child shall play over the hole of the cobra, and the weaned child shall put his hand on the adder's den. They shall not hurt or destroy in all my holy mountain; for the earth shall be full of the knowledge of the Lord as the waters cover the sea. In that day the root of Jesse, who shall stand as a signal for the peoples—of him shall the nations inquire, and his resting place shall be glorious.

Isaiah described the righteous leader as a King led by the spirit of YHWH and endowed with divine skills. The righteous leader submits to the Spirit of God and never acts as a law unto oneself.

Word Biblical Commentary explained that "righteousness and justice are elementary requirements of divine justice and royal rule."[2] The pericope highlights seven spiritual gifts endued to the righteous leader as outlined in pairs to include:

The Spirit of Wisdom and Understanding: Wisdom means the quality that enables the leader to make good judgments and quality decisions. Understanding reflects the deeper intellectual insight into the events and persons that are required to establish just policies.[3]

The Spirit of Counsel and Might: Counsel deals with the gift of forming right conclusions. Might represents the ability to execute with energy.[4]

The Spirit of Knowledge and the Fear of the Lord: Knowledge of YHWH refers to a true understanding and relation to God and His will. Fear of YHWH depicts the basic awe and submission of the leader to the Holy God who, in mystery beyond understanding, only gets worshipped.[5]

Leaders who follow the Spirit of God operate with a level of spiritual endowment that manifests skills beyond the knowledge of secular leaders. Daniel 1:19–20 reads,

> The king talked with them, and out of them all not one was found like Daniel, Hananiah, Mishael and Azariah; so they entered the king's personal service. As for every matter of wisdom and understanding about which the king consulted them, he found them ten times better than all the magicians and conjurers who were in all his realm.

The seven spiritual gifts empower the leader to demonstrate skills and potential above the naturally or academically trained leader.

> THE RIGHTEOUS LEADER SUBMITS TO THE SPIRIT OF GOD AND NEVER ACTS AS A LAW UNTO ONESELF.

Spiritually formed leaders follow the directives of God as the ultimate authority instead of their intellectual wisdom. As a result, spiritually formed leaders become equipped to achieve high levels of performance that increases notoriety and causes a paradigm shift in the marketplace. A meta-ethical theory known as, Divine Command Theory (DCT) claims that "God's insight is flawless and preeminent; God's character embodies love and justice deserving of the highest level of respect and all directives from God must be honored as a moral responsibility."[6] Solomon represents a biblical example of divine wisdom leading to influence and notoriety. The Book of First Kings 4:29–30 reports, *"Now God gave Solomon wisdom and very great discernment and breadth of mind, like the sand that is on the seashore. Solomon's wisdom surpassed the wisdom of all the sons of the east and all the wisdom of Egypt."* Solomon became known throughout the world as a righteous leader with great wisdom that attracted other kingdoms to seek his advice. First Kings 10:23–24 states, *"So King Solomon exceeded all the kings of the earth for riches and for wisdom. And all the earth sought to Solomon, to hear his wisdom, which God had put in his heart."* Solomon operated in a level of wisdom that astonished the world. He served as a righteous king who judged fairly, treated his employees favorably, and used spiritual discernment in making his difficult decisions.

Followers trust leaders to make accurate and fair decisions in settling disputes. Solomon navigated a difficult case in First Kings 3:16–28 proving the importance of discernment as a key skill for a leader.

> SPIRITUALLY FORMED LEADERS FOLLOW THE DIRECTIVES OF GOD AS THE ULTIMATE AUTHORITY INSTEAD OF THEIR INTELLECTUAL WISDOM.

Then two women who were harlots came to the king and stood before him. The one woman said, "Oh, my lord, this woman and I live in the same house; and I gave birth to a child while she was in the house. It happened on the third day after I gave birth, that this woman also gave birth to a child, and we were together. There was no stranger with us in the house, only the two of us in the house. This woman's son died in the night, because she lay on it. So she arose in the middle of the night and took my son from beside me while your maidservant slept, and laid him in her bosom, and laid her dead son in my bosom. When I rose in the morning to nurse my son, behold, he was dead; but when I looked at him carefully in the morning, behold, he was not my son, whom I had borne." Then the other woman said, "No! For the living one is my son, and the dead one is your son." But the first woman said, "No! For the dead one is your son, and the living one is my son." Thus they spoke before the king. Then the king said, "The one says, 'This is my son who is living, and your son is the dead one'; and the other says, 'No! For your son is the dead one, and my son is the living one.'" The king said, "Get me a sword." So they brought a sword before the king. The king said, "Divide the living child in two, and give half to the one and half to the other." Then the woman whose child was the living one spoke to the king, for she was deeply stirred over her son and said, "Oh, my lord, give her the living child, and by no means kill him." But the other said, "He shall be neither mine nor yours; divide him!" Then the king said, "Give the first woman the living child, and by no means kill him. She is his mother." When all Israel heard of the judgment which the king had handed down, they feared the king, for they saw that the wisdom of God was in him to administer justice.

Solomon utilized spiritual wisdom and discernment to adjudicate a difficult case. The preponderance of fake news in our contemporary society attempts to replace truth with fiction and places a higher demand for discernment as an essential skill for effective leadership. Too many leaders make ill-informed decisions by relying solely on their natural intellect and failing to apply spiritual intelligence. Right understanding leads to right decision-making. The United States waged war on Iraq based on erroneous information that claimed the existence of weapons of mass destruction. The Book of Daniel, chapter six, outlines how king Darius received faulty information causing him to sign legislation to regulate when and to whom to pray resulting in a death sentence for Daniel. Proverbs 29:12 NLT reads, *"If a ruler pays attention to liars, all his advisers will be wicked."* Leaders must use spiritual wisdom to assess situations and detect the motives of informers to discern the truth to make just decisions.

> RIGHT UNDERSTANDING LEADS TO RIGHT DECISION-MAKING

Leadership researchers explained a concept known as "bounded rationality approach" to mean that leaders make decisions with limited information and insufficient alternatives.[7] The bounded rationality approach results in leaders making quick decisions, failing to consider the pros and cons as well as the motives of influencers that contribute to the decision-making process. The verse in the pericope, from Isaiah 11, states that *"He shall not judge by what his eyes see, or decide disputes by what his ears hear.*" The righteous ruler judges a case beyond the surface and utilizes supernatural insight discerning right from wrong and good from evil. Oswalt asserted, "A human judge can do no more than to make the best use of his or her natural faculties in attempting to reach a fair ruling...Somehow this king [the righteous ruler] will go deeper than that and will pierce beneath appearances to the underlying reality"[8] Consequently, age and experience no longer predict wisdom as reiterated in Job 32:6–10 in *The Message* translation:

> TRUE WISDOM COMES FROM THE SPIRIT OF GOD.

> This is what Elihu, son of Barakel the Buzite, said: "I'm a young man, and you are all old and experienced. That's why I kept quiet and held back from joining the discussion. I kept thinking, 'Experience will tell. The longer you live, the wiser you become.' But I see I was wrong—it's God's Spirit in a person, the breath of the Almighty One that makes wise human insight possible. The experts have no corner on wisdom; getting old doesn't guarantee good sense. So I've decided to speak up. Listen well! I'm going to tell you exactly what I think.

Leaders tend to rely on experience or industry knowledge as the primary source of wisdom. Disruptive innovators discern revolutionary opportunities, and spiritually alert leaders find new solutions to entrenched problems that astound experienced experts. True wisdom comes from the Spirit of God, a supernatural force beyond the bounds of the natural intellect.

The scriptures provide multiple examples of how God empowered leaders with the seven gifts of the Spirit to perform exploits in the marketplace. In Genesis, chapter 41, Joseph used spiritual discernment to develop the strategic plan and forecast warning Pharaoh to preserve resources in the time of plenty in preparation for an impending famine. Joseph's plan preserved the economy and elevated Egypt to serve as the primary distributor of resources during the time of famine. Daniel outwitted all the secular experts in interpreting the dreams of King Nebuchadnezzar. Daniel 5:12 reads, *"Forasmuch as an excellent spirit, and knowledge, and understanding, interpreting of dreams, and shewing of hard sentences, and dissolving of doubts, were found in the same Daniel, whom the king named Belteshazzar: now let Daniel be called, and he will shew the interpretation."* The secular leaders failed to surrender to the Spirit of God thus unable to access the spiritual gifts of wisdom and understanding. In Second Kings, chapter six, Elijah's assistant became afraid as his natural eyes observed that the king of Aram sent troops, horses, and chariots to surround them. However, Elijah prayed to God on behalf of his servant to receive the spiritual sight to discern God's protection. Second Kings 6:15–17 reads,

> Now when the attendant of the man of God had risen early and gone out, behold, an army with horses and chariots was circling the city. And

> RIGHTEOUS LEADERS POSSESS TOP-LEVEL CLEARANCE TO RECEIVE SPIRITUAL DAILY INTELLIGENCE BRIEFINGS.

his servant said to him, "Alas, my master! What shall we do?" So he answered, "Do not fear, for those who are with us are more than those who are with them." Then Elisha prayed and said, "O LORD, I pray, open his eyes that he may see." And the LORD opened the servant's eyes and he saw; and behold, the mountain was full of horses and chariots of fire all around Elisha.

The time for righteous leadership has come. The world needs spiritual insight to combat the difficult problems of violence, inequality, injustice, poverty, and sickness in the world today. Righteous leaders possess top-level clearance to receive spiritual daily intelligence briefings to make quality decisions as noted in the two scriptures below:

1 Corinthians 2:6–8 King James Version (KJV)

Howbeit we speak wisdom among them that are perfect: yet not the wisdom of this world, nor of the princes of this world, that come to nought: But we speak the wisdom of God in a mystery, even the hidden wisdom, which God ordained before the world unto our glory: Which none of the princes of this world knew: for had they known it, they would not have crucified the Lord of glory.

1 Corinthians 2:13–15 King James Version (KJV)

> GOD ANOINTS AND APPOINTS THE RIGHTEOUS LEADER.

Which things also we speak, not in the words which man's wisdom teacheth, but which the Holy Ghost teacheth; comparing spiritual things with spiritual. But the natural man receiveth not the things of the Spirit of God: for they are foolishness unto him: neither can he know them, because they are spiritually discerned. But he that is spiritual judgeth all things, yet he himself is judged of no man.

Open your spiritual eyes and see that God equips and supports the spiritually formed leader to discern the right course of action to promote justice, peace, and prosperity for all including the most vulnerable in our society. To stop the corruption and abuse of power among unrighteous leaders, a generation of righteous leaders must take courage to arise and lead. God anoints and appoints the righteous leader. Isaiah 61:1–4 states,

The Spirit of the Lord GOD is upon me; because the LORD hath anointed me to preach good tidings unto the meek; he hath sent me to bind up the brokenhearted, to proclaim liberty to the captives, and the opening of the prison to them that are bound; To proclaim the acceptable year of the LORD, and the day of vengeance of our God; to comfort all that mourn; To appoint unto them that mourn in Zion, to give unto them beauty for ashes, the oil of joy for mourning, the garment of praise for the spirit of heaviness; that they might be called trees of righteousness, the planting of the LORD, that he might be glorified. And they shall build the old wastes, they shall raise up the former desolations, and they shall repair the waste cities, the desolations of many generations.

Isaiah prophesied that the righteous leader creates a seismic shift in a society designed to cause realignment to just and fair governance. The time to rise and rebuild cities and alleviate poverty through righteous leadership begins now!

[1]Oswalt, J. (1986). The Book of Isaiah, Chapters 1-39. In *The New International Commentary on the Old Testament*. Grand Rapids, Michigan: Wm. B. Eerdmans Publication Company.

[2]Watts, J. (2005). Isaiah 1-33. In *Word Biblical Commentary* (Vol. 24). Nashville: Thomas Nelson.

[3]Ibid.

[4]Keil, C., & Delitzsch, F. (1996). *Commentary on the Old Testament* (Vol. 7). Peabody, MA: Hendrickson.

[5]Watts, J. (2005). Isaiah 1-33. In Word Biblical Commentary (Vol. 24). Nashville: Thomas Nelson.

[6]Piazza, J., & Landy, J. F. (2013). "Lean not on your own understanding": Belief that morality is founded on divine authority and non-utilitarian moral judgments. *Judgment & Decision Making*, 8(6), 639-661.

[7]Ivancevich, J. M., Matteson, M. T., & Konopaske, R. (2011). *Organizational behavior and management* (Vol. 9). New York, NY: McGraw-Hill.

[8]Oswalt, J. (1986). The Book of Isaiah, Chapters 1-39. In *The New International Commentary on the Old Testament*. Grand Rapids, Michigan: Wm. B. Eerdmans Publication Company.

CHAPTER TWO KEY POINTS

- The righteous leader reverences God.

- People prosper when the righteous governs.

- Seven spiritual gifts empower the righteous leader to make quality decisions.

    1. The Spirit of the Lord

    2. The Spirit of Wisdom

    3. The Spirit of Understanding

    4. The Spirit of Counsel

    5. The Spirit of Might

    6. The Spirit of Knowledge

    7. The Fear of the Lord

- The wisdom of God supersedes the natural man's intellect.

- Spiritual intelligence enables the power of discernment to acquire the right understanding to make right decisions.

LIFE APPLICATION EXERCISES

Meditate Isaiah 11:2 for the next seven days.

_____

_____

Assess yourself and other leaders based on the
evidence of the seven spiritual gifts.

_____

_____

What insight did you receive and act upon based on
spiritual discernment?

_____

_____

List three distinguishing outcomes resulting from a
righteous versus an unrighteous leader.

_____

_____

List three characteristics of a righteous leader?

_____

_____

THE TOKEN LEADER

Also I heard the voice of the Lord, saying, Whom shall I send, and who will go for us? Then said I, Here am I; send me.

Isaiah 6:8

God assigns the believer to strategic places in society to stand in the gap for the disenfranchised and less powerful. For centuries society fails to acknowledge the evils of oppression and suppression of diverse engagement across people groups. The atrocities of Hitler oppressing the Jews, South African apartheid, and the Global Slave Trade provided only a few historical accounts where hatred and oppression yielded suboptimal results for society. Godly leaders must awaken and stand in the gap in schools, churches, businesses, governments and all spheres of influence. The Book of Esther serves as an exemplar case of the intergroup conflict between minority and majority groups in society and the important role of a token leader. A token leader means an influential leader positioned to bridge the gap between the majority power brokers and the minority group members. According to Esther 2:5–7 NASB, Mordecai, raised his orphaned cousin Esther, as his own daughter.

A TOKEN LEADER BRIDGES THE GAP BETWEEN THE MAJORITY AND THE MINORITY GROUP MEMBERS.

Now there was at the citadel in Susa a Jew whose name was Mordecai, the son of Jair, the son of Shimei, the son of Kish, a Benjamite, who had been taken into exile from Jerusalem with the captives who had been exiled with Jeconiah king of Judah, whom Nebuchadnezzar the king of Babylon had exiled. He was bringing up Hadassah, that is Esther, his uncle's daughter, for she had no father or mother. Now the young lady was beautiful of form and face, and when her father and her mother died, Mordecai took her as his own daughter.

Mordecai changed Esther's Jewish name Hadassah to Esther as a means of assimilating in the Persian culture. The Jewish people appeared to fully integrate into the Persian society by adopting the practices of the dominant culture. Esther 2:10 ESV stated, "Esther had not made known her people or kindred, for Mordecai had commanded her not to make it known." Mordecai's meticulous plan successfully assimilated Esther into the dominant Persian culture to the point that Esther became Queen of Persia. Although Esther remained incognito, Mordecai's conflict with Haman exposed her heritage and awakened her God-given destiny to deliver the Jewish people.

The Persian government issued a declaration that violated the traditions of the Jewish people. Mordecai's decision to adhere to his tradition exposes him and the entire Jewish race to retaliation. Esther 3:1–6 NASB provides the context for the conflict,

> After these events King Ahasuerus promoted Haman, the son of Hammedatha the Agagite, and advanced him and established his authority over all the princes who were with him. All the king's servants who were at the king's gate bowed down and paid homage to Haman; for so the king had commanded concerning him. But Mordecai neither bowed down nor paid homage. Then the king's servants who were at the king's gate said to Mordecai, "Why are you transgressing the king's command?' Now it was when they had spoken daily to him and he would not listen to them, that they told Haman to see whether Mordecai's reason would stand; for he had told them that he was a Jew. When Haman saw that Mordecai neither bowed down nor paid homage to him, Haman was filled with rage. But he disdained to lay hands on Mordecai alone, for they had told him who the people of Mordecai were; therefore Haman sought to destroy all the Jews, the people of Mordecai,

who were throughout the whole kingdom of Ahasuerus.

Haman served as prime minister next in command to the king. Haman possessed great wealth as he offered to add to the king's treasury stating, *"I will pay 10,000 talents of silver into the hands of those who have charge of the king's business, that they may put it into the king's treasuries"* (Esther 3:9 ESV). Mordecai's refusal to bow agitated Haman's ego. The saga of the relationship conflict between Haman and Mordecai escalated to hostile defiance and abuse of power in that he issued an edict to confer genocide upon the Jewish people. Haman leveraged his influence to manipulate the king to believe that a group of unnamed people presented a threat to the king's welfare.[1] Haman failed to disclose specific information about the plan to annihilate the Jewish people but rather appealed to the king's trepidation and sense of racial supremacy coupled with the enticement of a big financial payoff.[2] The relationship conflict between Mordecai and Haman led to an entrenchment of disagreement that required the token leader's intervention in the intergroup conflict.

Mordecai needed Esther to urgently intervene with the king to prevent great harm to the Jewish people. Esther 4:8 ESV states,

> Mordecai also gave him a copy of the written decree issued in Susa for their destruction, that he might show it to Esther and explain it to her and command her to go to the king to

beg his favor and plead with him on behalf of her people.

Esther found herself in a conundrum at the risk of revealing her identity to the king and the imminent need to intervene on behalf of her subgroup, the Jewish people. Esther explained the real danger to Mordecai stating in Esther 4:11 ESV that,

> "All the king's servants and the people of the king's provinces know that if any man or woman goes to the king inside the inner court without being called, there is but one law—to be put to death, except the one to whom the king holds out the golden scepter so that he may live. But as for me, I have not been called to come in to the king these thirty days."

The discourse between Mordecai and Esther grew intense. Mordecai explained that despite the efforts to assimilate in the Persian culture and the inroads in gaining status and acceptance as a member of the in-group, all members of the minority population including Esther risk death. In Esther 4:13 ESV, Mordecai replied to Esther stating,

> "Do not think to yourself that in the king's palace you will escape any more than all the other Jews. For if you keep silent at this time, relief and deliverance will rise for the Jews from another place, but you and your father's house will perish. And who knows whether you have not come to the kingdom for such a time as this?"

The escalation and gravity of the conflict led Esther to intervene to preserve the life of the Jewish people. The pericope found in Esther 7:3–6 ESV states:

> Then Queen Esther answered, "If I have found favor in your sight, O King, and if it please the king, let my life be granted me for my wish, and my people for my request. For we have been sold, I and my people, to be destroyed, to be killed, and to be annihilated. If we had been sold merely as slaves, men and women, I would have been silent, for our affliction is not to be compared with the loss to the king." Then King Ahasuerus said to Queen Esther, "Who is he, and where is he, who has dared to do this?" And Esther said, "A foe and enemy! This wicked Haman!" Then Haman was terrified before the king and the queen.

In addition to Esther's promotion to queen, Esther 2:21 noted that *"Mordecai was sitting at the king's gate"* (ESV). Both Esther and Mordecai attained leadership positions in Persia.

The Jewish people assimilated to the Persian culture and Haman knowingly omitted the people group he wished to destroy. Mordecai needed the intervention of someone in a higher position to access the king. Previously, Mordecai discovered the plot that endangered the king's life but still needed Esther to inform the king on his behalf. The disparity in power, wealth, and access left Mordecai and the Jewish people in need of a leader to intercede with the king to thwart the impending danger of extinction.

Rosabeth Moss Kanter developed the theory of proportional rarity with a focus on Tokenism in 1977.[3] Tokenism refers to "a situation in which individuals of one social group (i.e., women) are in extreme minority – less than 15 percent of the organization."[4] Kanter expressed that women operating as minorities in an organization face three issues: (a) *heightened visibility* meaning that mistakes become more apparent and carry greater consequences; (b) *contrast* deals with the social isolation, getting barred from informal gatherings, and treated as a misfit; and (c) *assimilation* refers to the token displaying characteristics that confirm the stereotypical biases of the dominant group.[5] In contemporary context, the election of Barack Obama to the presidency of the United States of America serves as an example of tokenism in that society considers him a part of the minority class yet voted for him to serve in a position of power and influence consistent with the majority class. The perceived change in the power structure threatens the status quo and creates relationship conflicts at various levels of society. Consequently, a token leader assimilating to a dominant culture remains susceptible to harm by malevolent members. The national debate in America about the role of race and racism reflects the tension and challenges of tokenism. Tokens feel the pressure to perform in excellence without becoming

> TOKENS FEEL THE PRESSURE TO PERFORM IN EXCELLENCE.

a threat to the dominant group. Also, token leaders serve as arbitrators and doorkeepers for admitting other minority members to join the dominant group. As a result, tokens risk losing the support of minority members while facing challenges from the dominant group. Societies and organizations must address issues of diversity in a responsible manner to avoid conflict that leads to destructive actions such as war, tribalism, and hate. According to First Peter 2:9 NASB, the Bible clearly indicates that God selected a subset of society stating, *"But you are a Chosen Race, A Royal Priesthood, A Holy Nation, A People for God's Own Possession, so that you may proclaim the excellencies of Him who has called you out of darkness into His marvelous light."*

Esther attained great status as a result of integrating into the Persian-dominant culture by hiding her heritage. Esther must now face the reality that tokens lack exemption and the fate of the Jewish people will affect her equally. Esther must utilize the power and status endued by God to intervene on behalf of her subgroup otherwise face death. Esther exercised great courage in making the decision to intervene on behalf of the Jewish people. Esther informed Mordecai to *"go gather all the Jews to be found in Susa, and hold a fast on my behalf, and do not eat or drink for three days night or day, I and my young women will also fast as you do"* (Esther 4:16a ESV). Esther demonstrated great leadership ability and courage and informed Mordecai that at the end of the fast, *"I will go to the king, though it is against the law, and if I perish, I perish"* (Esther 4:16b ESV). Esther realized that whether death by Haman or the king, the situation necessitated intervention on behalf of the Jewish people despite the risk. The risk of extinction due to Haman's malevolent act converted Esther to become a revolutionist. Esther activated the power placed in her by relying on divine assistance to intervene on behalf of her subgroup.

Esther applied effective leadership skills to intervene in the situation. Many born-again believers with power and authority in their respective spheres of influence fail to exercise courage to intervene in troubling situations. However, after Esther and the minority group completed the fast, Esther operated in divine wisdom in approaching the king. Esther 5:1 states that Esther adorned in her royal robe approached the king and requested favor. The king granted Esther favor and with discretion, good judgment, and skill, she requested a banquet and extended an invitation to Haman. Esther 5:4 outlined Esther's plan requesting, *"If it please the king, let the king and Haman come today to a feast that I have prepared for the king"* (ESV). Esther considered the recent promotion of Haman and used the opportunity to extend an invitation for a private feast. Esther intervened utilizing a measured strategy that allowed time to disarm both the king and Haman. In fact, the king asked Esther twice to disclose her request but without any visible anxiety, she patiently responded to the king by stating, *"...let the king and Haman come to the feast that I will prepare for them, and tomorrow I will do*

DUE TO HER OBEDIENCE TO GOD'S TIMING AND METHODS, THE DIVINE INTERVENED.

as the king has said" (Esther 5:8b ESV). Esther relied on divine assistance and acted patiently. Esther exercised discipline and emotional intelligence by reading the context and the gravity of her concern to establish the right environment to address her concerns. Due to her obedience to God's timing and methods, the Divine intervened in the interim. God reminded the king that Mordecai saved his life.

The moment Haman planned to execute his strategy by gaining approval from the king to kill Mordecai, God intervened. The king inquired of Haman how to bestow honor on someone. Haman, assuming the king desired to honor him, devised a lavish plan. However, the king revealed he desired to honor Mordecai for saving his life, thus averting Haman's plan to kill Mordecai and the Jews. Esther 6:10 outlined, *"Then the king said to Haman, 'Hurry; take the robes and the horse, as you have said, and do so to Mordecai the Jew, who sits at the king's gate"* (ESV). Continuing in verse 11, Haman, the enemy *"dressed Mordecai and led him through the square of the city, proclaiming before him, 'Thus shall it be done to the man whom the king delights to honor."* The perfect form of honor designed by Haman became Mordecai's reward.

> GOD FIGHTS BATTLES AND SECURES THE VICTORY.

God intervened and caused the enemy to bestow honor on his chosen, Mordecai the Jew. Real honor comes from God to the point that Haman, the powerful leader and the second in command to the king, now must experience public humiliation and honor Mordecai. The scripture states that

"Haman hurried to his house, mourning and with his head covered" (Esther 6:12 ESV). Haman's wife proclaimed that *"If Mordecai, before whom you have begun to fall, is of the Jewish people, you will not overcome him but will surely fall before him"* (Esther 6:13b ESV). Sadly, the overwhelming support once given to Haman to proceed with his plan to hang Mordecai now prophesies of his dismal fate. As such, the second day of the feast arrived and Esther informed the king of Haman's plot to destroy the Jewish people. The king ordered the death of Haman. Interestingly, one of the king's attending eunuchs informed the king that Haman prepared the gallows for Mordecai, so the king ordered Haman to face the dreadful fate he planned for Mordecai. The scriptures clearly illustrate that God fights the battle and secures the victory for the believer as well as reinforces the fact that only God can bestow real power, status, and honor.

The courage of Esther and the intervening power of God created a cultural shift that embraced diversity and empowered the minority group to revoke unjust laws. As a result of the disclosure of the full information to the king of Haman's plan, the minority group provided a perspective that altered the decision. According to Esther 8:11, the king permitted the Jews in every city to *"gather and defend their lives, to destroy, to kill, and to annihilate any armed force of any people or province that might attack them, children and women included, and to plunder their goods"* (ESV). Effective diversity management requires justice and empowerment of diverse workgroups. The minority group provided an alternate course that empowered them to create a counterculture that respects a diverse group of people.

Essentially, the abuse of power from a dominant group member requires intervention from a respected and effective token leader with the influence and empathy to create change. Leaders who represent the minority group must take responsibility despite the risk to defend and intervene on behalf of injustice and abuse of power to harm others including minority group members. The characteristics of an effective leader such as Esther, requires good judgment and decorum to implement strategies successfully to resolve intergroup relationship conflict. The story of Esther demonstrated that as a token, assimilation and acceptance in the dominant culture still exposes a minority group member to the same level of discrimination despite the leader's status. Lastly, minority leaders desire to assimilate but the existence of injustice will alter the goal of the minority group to more aggressively create a safe environment inclusive of diverse perspectives.

---

[1]Bush, F. W. (1998). *Ruth, Esther: Word Biblical Commentary* (Vol. 9). Dallas: Word, Incorporated.

[2]Ibid

[3]Wallace, J. E., & Kay, F. M. (2012). Tokenism, organizational segregation, and coworker relations in law firms. *Social Problems*, (3), 389.

[4]Ibid

[5]Ibid

CHAPTER THREE KEY POINTS

- Leaders must effectively manage diversity in groups to avoid intergroup conflict.

- Token leaders must exhibit the courage to intervene and resolve the intergroup conflict between minority and majority groups.

- Prayer and fasting serve as tools to secure divine strategies to resolve intergroup relationship conflict.

- Leaders must remain open to listening to complaints about the abuse of power of trusted confidants.

LIFE APPLICATION EXERCISES

Describe the type of diversity in your group.

_____

_____

Identify at least three intergroup conflict areas.

_____

_____

Outline two distinct positions of those who hold a minority and a majority status in the group?

_____

_____

Commit to prayer and fasting to seek God's guidance on strategies to resolve the conflict.

_____

_____

Write the strategy you plan to employ and the role you plan to play to mitigate the conflict?

_____

_____

CHAPTER FOUR

THE PRINCIPLED FOLLOWER-LEADER

There shall no evil befall thee, neither shall any plague come nigh thy dwelling. For he shall give his angels charge over thee, to keep thee in all thy ways.

Psalm 91:10–11

The story of Daniel provides a framework to explore the principles of power and influence in group decision making. Leaders must discern the dangers of group-think and possess the emotional intelligence to avoid suboptimal outcomes. King Darius' decision ordering Daniel to face the death penalty using the lion's den as found in Daniel 6:1–28 demonstrates flawed decision making. King Darius suffered from cognitive dissonance when he learned that he erroneously signed an irreversible decree that resulted in his most valuable employee facing the death penalty. Understanding the intricate and complex game playing strategies of Machiavellian employees who manipulate and pervert the decision-making process becomes essential for effective leadership. Leaders must adopt a systematic approach, skillfully manage information, apply good judgment, and make good decisions to improve organizational outcomes.

The Book of Daniel, chapter 6, depicts exemplary group decision making and the use of power. Daniel, a Jew, was taken into captivity in his youth and chosen to receive training in the Babylonian king's palace (Daniel 1:3). Daniel informed his tutor that he preferred to eat a different meal plan than the other students (Daniel 1:9). With some reservation, the tutor agreed and in the end noticed that Daniel's appearance and performance were ten times better than the other students (Daniel 1:20). The king of Babylon, Nebuchadnezzar, had a dream that his staff was unable to interpret except Daniel petitioned his God for the answer and interpreted the king's dream. As a result, Nebuchadnezzar promoted Daniel as ruler of the province of Babylon and chief over the wise men (Daniel 2:48–49).

Nebuchadnezzar's son, Belshazzar became the next king and encountered mysterious handwriting on the wall that Daniel also interpreted (Daniel 5). Daniel was again promoted and became the third ruler in the kingdom (Daniel 5:27–30). King Belshazzar died, and another king became enthroned, King Darius (Daniel

5:30). King Darius restructured the leaders and identified three presidents to manage the kingdom with Daniel as one of them and 120 other local province rulers (Daniel 6:1–3). Daniel was found to manage King Darius' affairs with such excellence that the king planned to promote Daniel to manage the entire kingdom (Daniel 6:3). According to commentaries, Daniel's anticipated promotion caused the other leaders to become jealous.[1] A strong relationship with the leader means employees with a low-quality relationship may become jealous.

The other two presidents and the local province rulers joined together to propose an irrevocable law to King Darius that adversely affected Daniel's worship to his God (Daniel 6:6–9). The leaders informed the king of their unanimous support to establish a law that no one can serve any other god but the king for the next thirty days (Daniel 6:7). The leaders urged the king to sign the decree immediately, to make the law irrevocable, and to render the death penalty for any violation (Daniel 6:8). After the king signed the petition into law, the leaders informed the king that Daniel violated the law and must receive the appropriate punishment of the death penalty (Daniel 6:12–13). The king regretting his decision tried to rescue Daniel, but the leaders once again agreed that Daniel must face the death penalty using the lion's den without any way of escape (Daniel 6:14–15).

> EMPLOYEES WITH A LOW-QUALITY RELATIONSHIP MAY BECOME JEALOUS.

The king felt dismayed and with much dissonance prayed for Daniel's safety then affirmed his punishment and ordered Daniel to his death (Daniel 6:16–17). The king recognized that the law he signed was a bad decision, fasted all night and waited anxiously to learn of Daniel's fate and the outcome of his decision (Daniel 6:18). The next day, the king hastened to see if Daniel's God was able to spare his life (Daniel 6:20). Daniel experienced no harm, and the king felt relieved. The king ordered the death of the leaders that coerced him into signing an unjust law (Daniel 6:24). Finally, King Darius exercised his authority and established a decree that all the people of the kingdom must serve the God of Daniel (Daniel 6:26).

The use of power and influence in Daniel 6 played a critical role in forming the decision made by King Darius. Ivancevich, Konopaske, and Matteson described two ways to obtain organizational power, *interpersonal power* and *structural power* (p. 341). **Interpersonal power** includes five types of power (1) *legitimate power* based on a person's positional authority and office in an organization; (2) *reward power* refers to a person's ability to determine the level of incentive warranted for certain behavior; (3) *coercive power* refers to a person's ability to penalize behavior; (4) *expert power* refers to a person's technical expertise; and (5) *referent power* refers to admired personality traits.[2] **Structural power** deals with the organizational culture and social infrastructure relating to decision rights regarding (1) allocation of resources; (2) directing the decision making process; and (3) dissemination of information.[3]

The researchers also mentioned that political tactics used in group decision making such as *game playing* strategies as described by Henry Mintzberg represent the pursuit of power and the demise of competitors.[4] Tactics used to influence members of the organization include (1) engaging others in the planning process; (2) assure others that the options presented are most plausible options; (3) gain support through intrinsically motivating others; (4) create a feeling of indebtedness; (5) leverage the support of others to gain more support; (6) peer pressure; (7) positional intimidation; (8) guilt in questioning one's commitment; and (9) quick pro quo.[5]

The malevolent leaders did not have the positional authority to prevent Daniel's promotion. King Darius had the ultimate authority to decide on the organizational structure and promotion of leaders in the kingdom. However, the leaders manipulated King Darius to impede Daniel's promotion and to sway the decision outcome in their favor. The two presidents and the local province leaders exercised the positional power to secure a meeting and to propose new policies to the king. Instead, the leaders used their structural power to influence the decision-making process. As for the group dynamics, the perpetrator of the scheme likely used interpersonal power to garner support for the petition from peers and subordinates. Evidently, only a subset of the leaders met with the king because Daniel was not part of the group that presented the petition.

King Darius' low self-esteem and fragile ego made him susceptible to considering a petition that made his kingship equal to god. King Darius' need for admiration blinded his eyes to the Machiavellian nature of the leaders to obscure the real intent to harm Daniel. The king made an emotional decision rather than a rational decision and signed the injunction. King Darius made several errors: (1) failure to identify the problem that required the need for a petition; (2) failure to ask the "5-whys" to understand why the decision was imminent; and (3) failure to consider alternative solutions.[6] The rational decision-making process serves as a means to mitigate negative decision outcome.[7] Additionally, the king failed to consider why the leaders assembled the entire leadership team and secured unanimous support for a petition unbeknownst to him. Daniel 6:14 described King Darius as confounded by the decision, yet he ordered Daniel to face the death penalty. The king bewildered by the circumstances gave up eating and sleeping as he agonized over Daniel's safety and whether Daniel's God had the power to save him. King Darius considered the potential loss of Daniel as significant to the future welfare of his kingdom. In fact, the king was prepared to promote Daniel as his most senior leader second in command to the king. Daniel proved his indispensable skill to interpret visions far superior to the otherwise men in the kingdom. The king fasted all night believing that Daniel's God would protect Daniel from harm and provide the king the opportunity to make a better decision. Once the king confirmed that Daniel was safe, the king took an autocratic leadership stance and fully utilized his power by ordering the mendacious leaders and their households to face the death penalty as they had prescribed for Daniel (Daniel 6:24). The king finally realized the full spectrum of the context of the situation. As a result, the king ruled that all territory under his domain including Mede and Persia must worship the God of Daniel (Daniel 6:25–27).

King Darius had the opportunity to correct the error of his decision as a result of God's divine intervention. However, many managers must accept poorly made decisions that harm members of the organization and impair organizational growth. The story of Daniel shows some of the disadvantages of group decision making, but studies reveal that groups also improve the quality of decision making. King Darius had the opportunity to improve the quality of his decision by establishing clear goals and guidelines for group decision making. The awareness of the use of power and political game playing can impede the quality of decisions. Therefore, a leader must remain vigilant in gathering sufficient data to make informed decisions.

> THE USE OF POWER AND POLITICAL GAME PLAYING CAN IMPEDE THE QUALITY OF DECISIONS.

Information serves a critical role in helping leaders make sound and strategic decisions dealing with contractual arrangements for managing employees.[8] Misleading information sharing, unethical decision making and betrayal of trusted advisors have existed from biblical times and extend to our contemporary organizational context. Matthew 26:14–16 revealed how Judas Iscariot, one of Jesus' disciples betrayed his leader for financial gain. The Book of Daniel, chapter three, depicted the deceptive behavior of King Nebuchadnezzar's trusted advisors who coerced him to issue a decree to attempt to put Daniel's colleagues to their death by fire. In the Book of Esther, chapter three, Haman plotted to kill the Jews unbeknownst to King Ahasuerus. Group members who interact with selfish and egotistical motives such as a Machiavellian member limit collaboration and group productivity.[9]

Machiavellianism derived from the 16th-century expositor of the Prince, Nicolo Machiavelli, who depicted people as conniving, egocentric and mendacious.[10] Machiavellian employees lack appropriate interpersonal skills and tend to utilize methods of manipulation and deception to achieve personal advancement.[11] Machiavellians operate without moral boundaries, and people consider them perfidious, inconsiderate, and disruptive representing the opposite views of group norms.[12] Machiavellian employees sinuously and extemporaneously adjust to a variety of situations without exertion appearing calm and composed in challenging situations.[13] Machiavellians tend to prefer unstructured environments and are often skilled in interpreting physical gestures to discern subtle nuances in communication.[14] Machiavellian employees communicate in an argumentative and confrontational manner to their peers and tend to place demands on the superior to affirm a supportive culture.[15]

> MACHIAVELLIAN EMPLOYEES LACK APPROPRIATE INTERPERSONAL SKILLS.

A leader's decision about what is right or wrong depends on their level of moral development and moral identity as well as the employees. People who consider themselves holy and sacred make moral decisions based on "divine command."[16] Some religious believers attribute the origin of morality as established by God and not based on human intellect.[17] The Divine Command Theory (DCT) claims that God's insight is flawless and preeminent; God's character embodies love and justice deserving of the highest level of respect, and adherence to all directives from God reflect honor and moral responsibility.[18] Religious people follow the leading of God as the ultimate authority and not their wisdom. Believers who work in a secular environment and unbelieving managers must recognize the risk of malevolent coworkers.

Believers must trust in knowing that promotion comes from God. In John 15:1–29, the pericope describes the role Jesus plays as the vine and vinedresser to cause the Believer to bear much fruit. The pericope highlights the importance of an employee's relationship with the leader. An employee who develops a high-quality relationship with the leader gains access to greater opportunities, rewards and positive performance evaluations. A mutually positive relationship between the employee and the leader provides the right environment to deliver corrective and constructive feedback to the employee that results in increased performance and organizational commitment.

> GOD'S INSIGHT IS FLAWLESS AND PREEMINENT.

In the pericope found in John 15:1–17, the text highlights the importance of relationship building and the performance evaluation process of correcting, developing and rewarding the follower. The text reveals the divine power of God and the Holy Spirit as key elements to improving follower performance and achieving organizational goals. The text describes the importance of abiding in the vine, referring to Jesus, as a means of becoming fruitful and productive (vv. 1–2). The scripture explains that God will remove unproductive efforts and dead-ends from the believer if a high-quality relationship exists (vv. 4–6). Jesus promises a blank check and unlimited favor if the believer obeys His commands (vv. 7–8). Jesus clarifies and makes transparent the motivation of the promise as the result of love and compassion (vv. 9–11). Jesus shared that the result of developing a high-quality relationship means that the believer becomes a co-laborer and partner with Jesus rather than a slave or contract worker (v. 15). The pericope epitomizes the benefits an employee derives from developing a high-quality relationship with the leader. Daniel developed such a strong relationship with God that he knew that God's protection resulted from obedience to his commandments even when they violate secular rules.

In the pericope, God makes himself known as the primary instrument for fruitfulness. God promises to care for and develop his people to become productive in every area of life. God requires a commitment to honor and obey his commands to reap the benefits of the relationship. John 15:5–6 reminds the believer that fruitfulness reflects a life of commitment to God's methods and purpose for the life of the believer. An effective prayer life, similar to Daniel, results in protection from evil and victory for every battle. A strong prayer life gives the believer access to innovative concepts and wisdom to produce supernatural results. Isaiah 54:17 reads that *"'No weapon that is formed against you will prosper; and every tongue that accuses you in judgment you will condemn. This is the heritage of the servants of the Lord, and their vindication is from Me,' declares the Lord* (NASB). Jesus promises a reward for obedience and a high-quality relationship of fellowship and prayer. God grants those who abide in him peace, joy, and love. The scripture promises that the fruit-bearing levels of the believer when abiding in God brings an increase in areas beyond material possessions. Jesus shows great love to the believer that reveals an intimacy with God that leads to promotion and recognition of supernatural favor and protection. Jesus promises to advocate and die for those who abide in him.

Belonging to the community of believers calls for a demonstration of loyalty in the midst of persecution from outsiders.

> GOD GRANTS THOSE WHO ABIDE IN HIM PEACE, JOY, AND LOVE.

The same hatred the world expressed towards Jesus gets directed to those who believe and abide in him. To follow Jesus requires a high degree of commitment.

Daniel served as a follower-leader as he submitted to the commandments of God. Despite the attacks and hardships imposed by malevolent co-workers and his misinformed boss, Daniel's commitment to God preserved him. The believer must remain steadfast in challenging situations to uphold the integrity and principles of the kingdom of God. The decision to withhold a vote and take a stand of justice reflects the character and fortitude to obey God's command over the popular trends that violate God's Word. Standing firm in prayer and trusting in God brings protection from harm and glorifies God in the end. Leaders must exercise the discipline and discernment to gather information from all sources transparently and openly to avoid erroneous decision making.

---

[1]Baldwin, J. G. (1978). *Daniel: An Introduction and Commentary* (Vol. 23, pp. 140-146). Downers Grove, IL: InterVarsity Press.

[2]Ivancevich, J. M., Matteson, M. T., & Konopaske, R. (2011). *Organizational behavior and management* (Vol. 9). New York, NY: McGraw-Hill.

[3]Ibid, pp. 343-345

[4]Ibid, pp. 354

[5]Ibid, pp. 354-355

[6]Ibid, pp. 411-413

[7]Ibid, pp. 410

[8]Stolowy, H., Messner, M., Jeanjean, T., & Richard Baker, C. (2014). The construction of a trustworthy investment opportunity: Insights from the Madoff fraud. *Contemporary Accounting Research*, 31(2), 354-397.

[9]Becker, J. A., & Dan O'Hair, H. (2007). Machiavellians' motives in organizational citizenship behavior. *Journal of Applied Communication Research*, 35(3), 246-267.

[10]Ibid, p. 251

[11]Ibid, p 248

[12]Ibid, p 248

[13]Ibid, p 251

[14]Ibid, p 251

[15]Walter, H. L., Anderson, C. M., & Martin, M. M. (2005). How subordinates' Machiavellianism and motives relate to satisfaction with superiors. *Communication Quarterly*, 53(1), 57-70.

[16]Piazza, J., & Landy, J. F. (2013). "Lean not on your own understanding": Belief that morality is founded on divine authority and non-utilitarian moral judgments. *Judgment & Decision Making*, 8 (6), 639-661.

[17]Ibid, p. 641

[18]Ibid, p. 641

Chapter Four Key Points

- Leaders must apply a systematic approach to gather adequate information in making good quality decisions.

- Leaders must discern and examine the motives of trusted advisors and influencers when making a decision.

- Employees utilize the interpersonal power and structural power to influence the decision-making process.

- Leaders must possess high levels of self-esteem to avoid manipulation by Machiavellian employees.

- Leaders must establish a culture that promotes transparency and honesty.

- Leaders must encourage input from all key leaders for critical decisions.

- Spiritually formed leaders trust in God's divine protection and ultimate authority to exercise justice in every situation.

LIFE APPLICATION EXERCISES

List and gather detailed information from all relevant personnel in making a decision.

_____

_____

Ask each leader to identify the pros and cons of the recommended solution.

_____

_____

Discern if the rationale for the solution strokes the leader's ego or promotes self-interest?

_____

_____

Meditate Psalm 91.

_____

_____

Schedule a mandatory meeting for individuals to publicly affirm the decision.

_____

_____

CHAPTER FIVE

FOUR VALUES OF LEADERSHIP

But the fruit of the Spirit is love, joy, peace, patience, kindness, goodness, faithfulness, gentleness, self-control; against such things there is no law.

Galatians 5:22–23

Values represent essential attributes to understand the ethical and moral character of a leader. The pericope found in Colossians 3:1–17 provides insights into how the first century Christian exhibited Christ-like values in the Greco-Roman culture. The four values explored include compassion, meekness, forgiveness, and humility. Amidst a leadership crisis, the need to understand and promote value-based leadership is of paramount importance. The Bible serves as a great resource to study values applicable to leadership principles and leader behavior. The pericope shares how Paul disciplines the believers in Colossae to have values that are consistent with a Christ-like lifestyle. Colossians 3:1–17 ESV reads as follows:

> If then you have been raised with Christ, seek the things that are above, where Christ is, seated at the right hand of God. Set your minds on things that are above, not on things that are on earth. For you have died, and your life is hidden with Christ in God. When Christ who is your life appears, then you also will appear with him in glory. Put to death therefore what is earthly in you: sexual immorality, impurity, passion, evil desire, and covetousness, which is idolatry. On account of these the wrath of God is coming. In these you too once walked, when you were living in them. But now you must put them all away: anger, wrath, malice, slander, and obscene talk from your mouth. Do not lie to one another, seeing that you have put off the old self with its practices and have put on the new self, which is being renewed in knowledge after the image of its creator. Here there is not Greek and Jew, circumcised and uncircumcised, barbarian, Scythian, slave, free; but Christ is all, and in all. Put on then, as God's chosen ones, holy and beloved, compas-

THE BIBLE SERVES AS A GREAT RESOURCE TO STUDY LEADERSHIP PRINCIPLES.

sionate hearts, kindness, humility, meekness, and patience, bearing with one another and, if one has a complaint against another, forgiving each other; as the Lord has forgiven you, so you also must forgive. And above all these put on love, which binds everything together in perfect harmony. And let the peace of Christ rule in your hearts, to which indeed you were called in one body. And be thankful. Let the word of Christ dwell in you richly, teaching and admonishing one another in all wisdom, singing psalms and hymns and spiritual songs, with thankfulness in your hearts to God. And whatever you do, in word or deed, do everything in the name of the Lord Jesus, giving thanks to God the Father through him.

Colossians, chapter three, implores all Christians to take off the old man, old vices and put on the incarnated attributes of Christ. The believers in Colossae committed to the life of Jesus, the King who went to the cross and possesses all power. In the backdrop of the counter-culture of believers Paul encourages them to "put on" Christ-like virtues that differ from the secular world and align with the ethic that God requires of each leader. To be Christ-like, take off anger and malice and put on compassion, forgiveness, humility, and meekness.

Compassion

*The weight of the ball gets heavier when
placed in your hands then compassion fails
to become a sideline sport —A Proverb*

The Western culture represents a high sense of individualism and becoming a compassionate leader means to risk appearing weak or irresponsible to trade off productivity with compassion. The industrialized world cares more about some widgets produced rather than the people and the hearts that causes the companies to operate efficiently. Leaders experience a real tension between acting compassionate and driving for maximum productivity. Colossians 3:13 ESV reads, *"Put on then, as God's chosen ones, holy and beloved, compassionate hearts."* Compassion is caring for others in an active and meaningful way. Compassion consists of three components: (1) empathy or understanding the feelings of others; (2) caring for the other person (e.g., affiliative arousal); and (3) willingness to act in response to the person's feelings.[1] Boyatzis et al. posited that,

> Compassion is a way to offset the negative effects of power stress. For leaders to sustain themselves, the human response to stress must be ameliorated. We argue that the practice of coaching others for their development can have this effect. Coaching, along with the experience of compassion, should ameliorate the negative physiological and psychological effects of power

stress. In this way, coaching with compassion is likely to enhance a leader's sustainability.[2]

The leader becomes stressed in managing the perception of what others may think and whether the work will be completed well and on time. Imagine, when a single mother calls into work on the third day in a row requesting time away from work to care for a sick child, compassion becomes necessary but low organizational trust makes the situation awkward for leaders to establish boundaries. Recently a colleague was diagnosed with cancer, and after his extensive treatment, the company released him stating the position became defunct. He must learn to deal with the psychology and physiology challenges as a cancer survivor and actively seek new employment. Many leaders assume that granting compassion or becoming a compassionate leader puts them at risk to appear weak and vulnerable. Psalm 78:38 reads, *"But he, being full of compassion, forgave their iniquity, and destroyed them not: yea, many a time turned he his anger away, and did not stir up all his wrath."* The secular standard of leadership differs greatly from the godly mandate to show compassion to employees.

> COMPASSION IS A WAY TO OFFSET THE NEGATIVE EFFECTS OF POWER STRESS.

A popular television series titled, "Undercover Boss" reveals the impact when a boss gives up the corner office and luxury lifestyle to work among the line-level employees in the company, the CEO often learns about the extraordinary commitment and struggles of the average worker in the company. Inevitably, overwhelmed by the sacrifices the employees endure to contribute to the workplace the CEO becomes compassionate towards the employees. The boss often grants increased compensation or provide resources to help the employee overcome struggles such as reliable transportation, tuition assistance for employees and family members, paid vacation time, and promotions. The Undercover Boss TV show reveals that when the leader invests in getting to know their employees, trust, empathy, and compassion becomes a form of building community and trust. The employees respond positively to compassionate acts with a greater degree of loyalty and organizational commitment. At a minimum, a leader must willingly risk caring for others without considering self-interest and impression management as a factor. When the leader takes the time to become familiar with the hearts of the employees in the organization, compassion naturally follows as the outcome.

MEEKNESS

When you are ready to speak, think,
then speak softly – A Proverb

Meekness represents a key virtue for leaders who are responsible for managing and influencing others. Pettigrove asserted that "Meekness is the virtue whose purview is the governance of anger and related emotions...The meek person is slow to anger and is not prone to resent others, to desire their suffering, or to take pleasure in their distress."[3] Martin Luther King, Jr. was an exemplary leader who exhibited the virtue of meekness. Despite the injustices that he encountered, he handled most of the encounters with meekness and self-control resulting in him being a remarkable leader. Yukl explained that "leaders with low emotional stability are more prone to extreme mood swings or outbursts of anger."[4] Leaders hold a position of power and authority in an organization. Bullying and outbursts of anger can lead to demoralizing the staff. Winston pointed out that, "The meek leader corrects employees when necessary, but does so in a way that causes the employee to grow...Unprincipled leaders correct people in hurtful ways that leave emotional scars on the employee."[5]

Sadly as the United States starts another election season, one of the virtues to examine among the political candidates is meekness. A Congressman's outburst of anger in a publicly televised forum addressed the President of the United States rudely and brought shame on America. The statesman caused the world to

> THE MEEK PERSON IS SLOW TO ANGER.

question the Nation's decorum and political diplomacy in a public forum. Likewise, an unstable emotional leader can disrupt the harmony in an organization. Most importantly, the priorities to achieve organizational goals become subverted to the urgency of dealing with personality and character issues. Knights & O'Leary quoted that "Molyneaux (2003: 347) emphasizes 'meekness', which he argues is an important personal quality for highest-level leadership: 'meekness' is not about 'powers foregone' but 'powers controlled and exercised with discernment.'"[6] Jesus Christ who exercised great self-control even to his death serves as the greatest example of a meek leader. In contrast, Jesus' disciple, Peter exhibited such anger he severed the soldier's ear. Meekness requires for every leader to have the level of emotional stability only attained through deep spiritual maturity.

Forgiveness

Forgiveness is giving a gift to oneself – A Proverb

Forgiveness represents one of the virtues that yields one of the greatest benefits regarding self-awareness and personal development. Due to lack of forgiveness, nations continue to war against each other as a result of a grudge or malice from centuries or generations ago. Forgiveness ignores if someone admits wrongdoing. Forgiveness represents a transformative process that takes place in the person offended and not always the one who has caused the offense. Forgiveness reflects self-actualization in the ability to create inner peace despite the uncontrollable actions of others. Nelson quoted Klyne Snodgrass saying,

> What forgiveness does accomplish is the rejection of bitterness, malice, and revenge. We do not control the actions of others, but in choosing to forgive we establish control over our own responses. We choose to value the other person despite his or her offense and to desire what is good for that person before God. Forgiveness also restores relations, or at least provides a foundation on which they can be restored.[7]

Christ forgave us without requiring admission of wrongdoing. The ability to forgive is the medicine that provides the cure to the open wounds of offense. The Bible warns in Hebrews 12:15 NASB, *"See to it that no one comes short of the grace of God; that no root of bitterness springing up causes trouble, and by it many be defiled."* Forgiveness requires making a choice. Most people find forgiving others as a very difficult decision to make. Nelson stated,

> But, our vertical forgiveness is not automatically the result of our horizontal forgiveness. Nor is our horizontal forgiveness meritorious. Michael Wilkins rightly comments, "Those who have received forgiveness are so possessed with gratitude to God that they in turn will eagerly forgive those who are 'debtors' to them." Thus, our forgiveness of others is an expression of gratitude for the salvific forgiveness we have already received through faith in the atoning work of Christ.[8]

Nelson Mandela represents an exemplar of a person to whom injustice warrants offense yet he exhibited the fortitude to forgive.

> FORGIVENESS REFLECTS SELF-ACTUALIZATION.

Forgiveness benefits the one who forgives and not the oppressor. Nelson Mandela's freedom from offense and hate occurred when he forgave his oppressors and not a function of his release from prison. Proverbs 25:21–22 NASB states that *"If your enemy is hungry, give him food to eat; and if he is thirsty, give him water to drink; for you will heap burning coals on his head, and the Lord will reward you.*" Essentially, the Bible encourages us to love our enemies. The act of forgiveness towards someone responsible for doing you harm confuses the devil and his operatives. Love conquers all and covers a multitude of sins. Remember, that God forgives us despite the many times we fail to show gratitude for His kindness or the times we accuse Him of failing us. If we desire forgiveness from God, we must learn to forgive others and especially employees and co-workers who fail short of our expectations.

Forgiveness must become a key virtue in the workplace. Many employees operate in fear of making a mistake and thus fail to provide creative solutions and take appropriate risk. Leaders must create an environment of forgiveness for innovation and creativity to flourish to achieve stronger performance and reward for all. A forgiving culture builds community and trust across the organization. One of the most stressful activities in a dyadic relationship involves the performance appraisal process. The performance appraisal process in a low trust work environment infuses fear and allows for the offense to distract employees from high-level performance opportunities. Employees short-circuit their career growth due to an unmanaged offense. Employees become bitter toward employers as a result of poorly executed performance reviews. The lack of forgiveness leads to a downward spiral from an employer's lack of trust to an employee's bad attitude resulting in declining performance and eventual dismissal. Some

> GOD FORGIVES US DESPITE THE MANY TIMES WE FAIL.

employees become offended as a result of delayed or denied career advancement opportunities. Leaders must establish a culture of forgiveness.

Leaders must manage the performance review process as a coaching session rather than an assessment. Good coaches inform players of blind spots that hinder superior performance. Good coaches lead players to find the right environment and positions for achieving team goals. Employers and employees must establish high levels of trust that allows honest feedback to take place to achieve productivity and increase individually and collectively. Likewise, employees must proactively seek ways to pursue personal development opportunities to become more equipped for career growth. Forgiveness becomes a critical and essential attribute to create an atmosphere of creativity and innovation. Employers must convey to employees that mistakes and taking risk serve as stepping stones to innovation and not a career-ending curse. Forgiveness as a virtue transforms people and organizations and in the case of Nelson Mandela, forgiveness changed the world.

> **FORGIVENESS MUST BECOME A KEY VIRTUE IN THE WORKPLACE.**

HUMILITY

Humility leads sitting in the second chair – A proverb

In most organizations regardless of size or industry, finding humble people and more so humble leaders has become a rarity. In America, the era of self-branding and proliferation of social media has made humility a rare commodity. Preachers, teachers, and entertainers are in pursuit of fame and public recognition. Good deeds are no longer private acts of kindness but another public relations campaign to build a personal brand. Today, people give the honor with ease based on how many Twitter followers or Facebook friends you garner as a result effective self-promotion and self-aggrandizement. The fall of Enron, WorldCom, and Lehman Brothers occurred due to the leader's ego seeking the recognition as the fastest growing, largest and most profitable business in the industry. Gandhi serves as a great exemplar of humility. Low et al., quoted Gandhi stating that "Anyone, who would sacrifice his or her life for others has hardly time to reserve for him (her)self a place in the sun...True humility means most strenuous and constant endeavor, wholly intended towards the service of humanity."[9] Humility represents a virtue that when valued in an organization leads to strong teamwork. Humility minimizes internal competition and allows people to work with each other synergistically as one body to achieve a common objective.

> HUMILITY FUNCTIONS FROM THE HEART.

Conversely, too much or false humility yields similar results as a lack of humility. In an organization where too much humility exists produces a lack of accountability and responsibility. In religious organizations where humility reflects a valued virtue, people tend to avoid taking ownership, and thus problems linger and go unresolved. Humility functions from the heart. Humility emanates from the spirit. Morris et al. defined humility as "three connected but distinct dimensions including 1) self-awareness – objective appraisal of one's ability, 2) openness – open to new ideas and understanding one's limitations, and 3) transcendence – require belief in an omnipotent God. Authentic humility involves neither self-abasement nor overly positive self-regard."[10] Humility means to know and accept oneself without external affirmation. Several biblical stories demonstrated that a lack of humility ultimately leads to one's demise. Haman desired to exalt himself and secure honor from the king while secretly planning to kill Mordecai. As a result, Haman hung on the gallows he prepared for Mordecai. Proverbs 29:23 NASB reads that *"A man's pride will bring him low, but a humble spirit will obtain honor."* A lack of humility leads to harming others and in turn harming oneself. True leadership deals with caring for others and not the pursuit of self-interest. Leaders must exhibit humility in managing people and in decision-making.

In summary, the Christians of Colossae were challenged to operate in the fruit of the spirit deemed worthy for followers of Christ. The four values including compassion, meekness, forgiveness, and humility represent essential qualities in the development and growth of an exemplary and ethical leader. Furthermore, these values when adopted and practiced lead to a deeper relationship with Jesus Christ and a quality work environment designed to build trust, loyalty, superior performance, and team-work. Become a leader with the courage to lead with Christ-like values.

[1]Boyatzis, R. E., Smith, M. L., & Blaize, N. (2006). Developing Sustainable Leaders Through Coaching and Compassion. *Academy Of Management Learning & Education*, 5(1), 8-24. doi:10.5465/AMLE.2006.20388381

[2]Ibid, p. 12

[3]Pettigrove, G. (2012). Meekness and 'Moral' Anger. *Ethics*, 122(2), 341-370.

[4]Yukl, G. (2013). Leadership in organizations (8th ed.). Englewood Cliffs, N.J.: Prentice-Hall.

[5]Winston, B. (1997). *Be a Leader for God's Sake: From Values to Behaviors* (2002 ed.).Virginia Beach: Regent University School of Leadership Studies.

[6]Knights, D., & O'Leary, M. (2005). Reflecting on corporate scandals: the failure of ethical leadership. *Business Ethics: A European Review*,14(4), 359-366. doi:10.1111/j.1467-8608.2005.00417.x

[7]Nelson, R. A. (2012). Exegeting forgiveness. *American Theological Inquiry (Online)*, 5(2), p. 37

[8]Ibid, p. 42

[9]Low, P. C., Sik-Liong, A., & Robertson, R. W. (2012). Gandhi and His Value of Humility. *Leadership & Organizational Management Journal*, 2012(3), 105-116.

[10]Morris, J. A., Brotheridge, C. M., & Urbanski, J. C. (2005). Bringing humility to leadership: Antecedents and consequences of leader humility. *Human Relations*, 58(10), 1323. doi:10.1177/0018726705059929

Chapter Five Key Points

- God requires a leader to demonstrate Christ-like virtues such as compassion, forgiveness, humility, and meekness.

- Compassionate leaders show empathy toward employees by understanding the needs and challenges they face on a regular basis.

- Leaders must exhibit a meek temperament in managing challenging situations.

- Leaders and followers must guard against taking offense and choose to forgive regularly and consistently to avoid bitterness and promote a trusting work environment.

- Humility represents a key attribute for building strong teamwork and collaboration

LIFE APPLICATION EXERCISES

Show compassion towards someone today.

Identify three steps to exhibit meekness.

Forgive and ask for forgiveness from at least one person this week.

Demonstrate humility and servant leadership by assisting someone with a physical task.

Identify a leader with Christ-like virtues and the qualities you admire the most.

Conclusion

Do this, knowing the time, that it is already the hour for you to awaken from sleep; for now salvation is nearer to us than when we believed.

Romans 13:11 NASB

I pray this book awakens you to leadership. The compilation of the five essays reveals innovative and diverse approaches to effective leadership in difficult situations. To remain complacent and laissez-faire about the selection of our civic and business leaders as well as ignore the misdeeds of bad actors represent a blatant abdication of our duty as human beings. We must arise and speak up when unjust policies get enacted, or a fellow employee gets mistreated. The opportunity to rise to leadership surrounds us every day as we stand up for truth, defend the powerless, and respond to injustices we face or observe in life. We must become fearless and begin to acknowledge and activate the power within us and demand higher levels of moral leadership. A leader's submission to God unlocks spiritual gifts of discernment and wisdom to see opportunities and solve problems beyond the realm of the human intellect.

God's anointing rests upon you to fulfill His plan for humanity. As God favored Esther and delivered Daniel, He promises to do the same for you. The time to access the supernatural power of God begins with having the confidence in God. Second Corinthians 3:4–6 NASB reads, *"Such confidence we have through Christ toward God. Not that we are adequate in ourselves to consider anything as coming from ourselves, but our adequacy is from God."* The skills and confidence to lead comes from God and not our natural ability. As noted in chapter five, the values of compassion, humility, meekness, and forgiveness represent the attributes of Christ. The more we rely on His ability and guidance, the more we resemble Him in our deeds. Jesus showed courage to overcome every obstacle.

Leadership extends beyond positional authority and belongs to those who stand courageously for righteousness. Esther and Mordecai planned to live a life of obscurity by assimilating in the Persian culture until the risk of death compelled them to act. Decide to stop hiding and start trusting in God. Godly leadership requires that we care for others above concern for ourselves. Fear means to become self-centered and self-interested. Jesus decided to set aside His desires, and His thriving ministry to go the Cross to save humanity. Daniel took courage in facing the lions, and God delivered him. The anointing of God rests upon your life to empower you for fearless leadership. Remember, you win! Satan failed to outwit God, and you possess the Spirit of Wisdom and the various facets of the anointing of God to outwit malevolent and jealous adversaries. Mark 14:41b ESV reads, *"Are you still sleeping and taking your rest? It is enough; the hour has come…"* Across the globe, people go hungry, get bullied, and live in war zones due to unrighteous leaders. The hour to wake up and lead has come!

Connect With Deloris

- Facebook: /deloris.thomas.528

- Twitter: @DelorisSThomas

- Instagram: @delorissthomas

- Email: DelorisSThomas@gmail.com

NOTES

NOTES

NOTES

NOTES

Printed in Great Britain
by Amazon